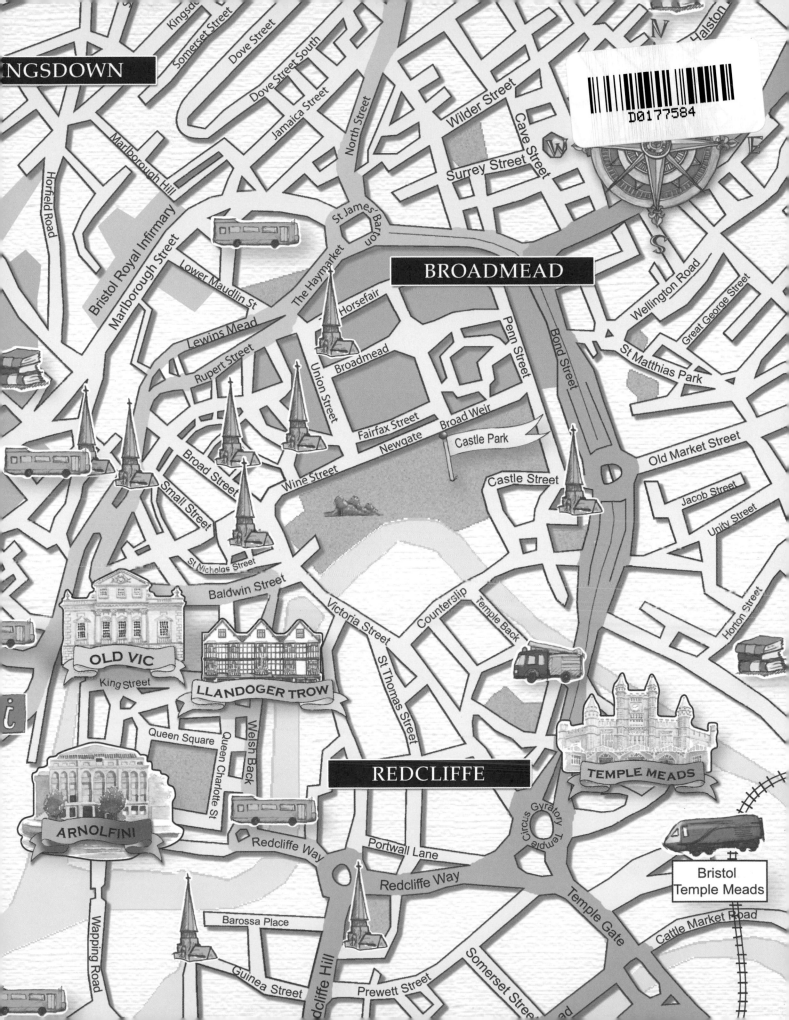

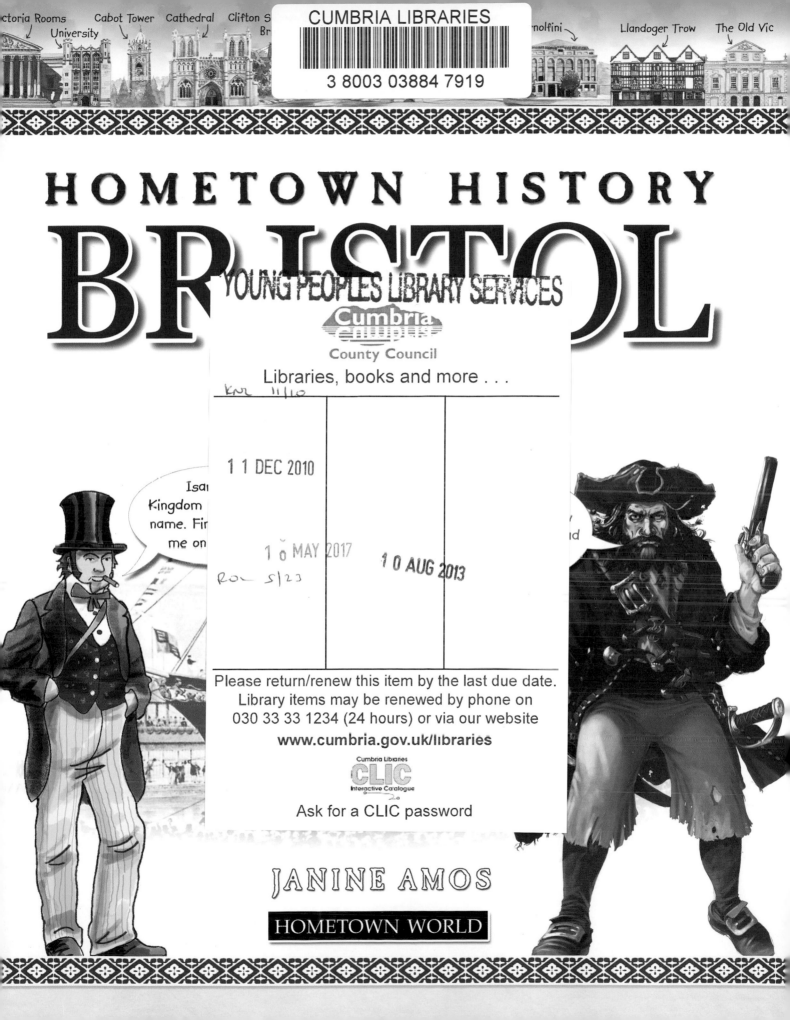

HOMETOWN HISTORY

BRISTOL

JANINE AMOS

HOMETOWN WORLD

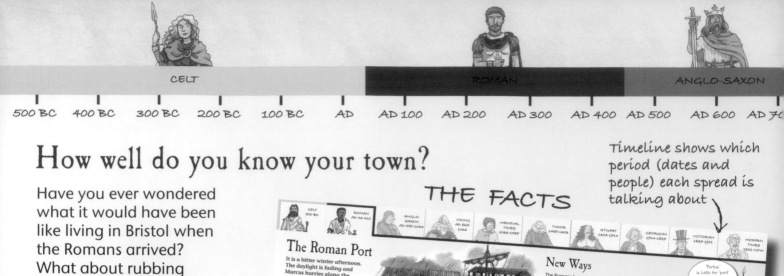
How well do you know your town?

Have you ever wondered what it would have been like living in Bristol when the Romans arrived? What about rubbing shoulders with the rich and famous in the Corn Exchange? This book will uncover the important and exciting things that happened in your town.

Want to hear the other good bits? You will love this book! Some rather brainy folk have worked on it to make sure it's fun and informative. So what are you waiting for? Peel back the pages and be amazed at what happened in your town.

Timeline shows which period (dates and people) each spread is talking about

Clear informative text

'Spot this!' game with hints on something to find in your town

Hometown facts to amaze you!

Intriguing old plans and photos

Go back in time to read what it was like for children growing up in Bristol

Each period in the book ends with a summary explaining how we know about the past

Contents

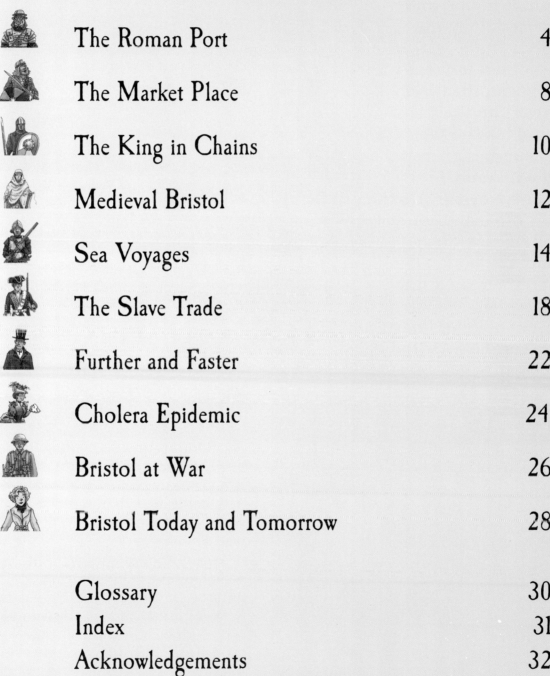

The Roman Port

It is a bitter winter afternoon. The daylight is fading and Marcus hurries along the road. His short tunic is made of warm wool but it doesn't protect him from the wind. Marcus shivers and pulls his cloak around him for warmth. His leather sandals are wet and caked with mud. Marcus is a merchant, travelling to the Roman port of Portus Abonae with finger-rings, brooches and necklaces to trade. He hopes to sell them all at the market. The smell of smoke reaches him. Cooking! Roasted chicken, or hare? Nearly there!

Roman Invasion

The Romans invaded Britain in AD 43 and settled here. The new Roman emperor Claudius wanted to show how powerful he was by taking over new lands. Britain had many things the Romans wanted, such as grain, iron, silver and gold, as well as hunting dogs, cattle and slaves.

Portus Abonae, at Sea Mills, lay about 6 kilometres downriver from what we know as Bristol today. Like Bristol, it was a port which the Romans used to supply their fort at Caerleon on the other side of the River Severn. A Roman road crossing Durdham Down connected Portus Abonae to Aquae Sulis (the Roman name for Bath). Some of the road crossed the Downs near Stoke Road and a short length can still be seen today as a grassy bank.

TUDOR
1485-1603

STUART
1603-1714

GEORGIAN
1714-1837

VICTORIAN
1837-1901

MODERN
TIMES
1902-NOW

New Ways

The Romans brought with them new ways of doing things. Paved roads, like the one unearthed at Durdham Down, replaced the muddy, pot-holed tracks linking towns. Merchants travelled from different parts of the Roman Empire to towns like Portus Abonae to buy and sell goods with Roman coins. The Romans introduced new ways of making pottery, glass and metal. They spoke Latin and even had their own numbers – Roman numerals.

Near Portus Abonae, the Romans built stone and brick villas, like the one you can still see at Kings Weston. These were large country houses or farms, often luxurious buildings, with underfloor heating and suites of baths. We can tell what people ate in Roman times from the bones, seeds and shells buried in the ground. Archaeologists have also dug up iron tools, pottery, bracelets, rings and pins and even skeletons!

> 'Portus' is Latin for 'port' and 'Abonae' comes from the Celtic word for 'rivers'.

> The Roman army didn't have toilet paper. They used a sponge soaked in water on the end of a stick instead!

> Sponge on a stick? That sounds painful!

Roman Briton

At the time of the Roman invasion, the people already living in Britain were called Britons. After the Roman conquest, most Britons worked on the land just as before and were still ruled by local chiefs. But slowly life began to change for everyone. The chiefs began to dress and speak Latin like the Romans. Stone and brick villas, like Kings Weston, replaced draughty wood and thatch forts. The Romans introduced their own gods and goddesses and the Britons came to worship these alongside their own gods and goddesses of nature and the seasons.

SPOT THIS!

This statue of Neptune represents the Roman god of the sea. Can you spot it in the city centre?

No one knows who lived in the villa at Kings Weston. Here is an imaginary diary written by 10-year-old Amicus whose family is wealthy enough to live in a villa. How was his life in Roman times different from your life today?

> Tabula is like the game backgammon that you play today.

Dies Lunae (Monday)

Today we must be very quiet in the villa. My little sister Vellibia is ill. Mother sits next to her, stroking her hair and burning bay leaves to help her sleep. Father has sent one of our slaves to bring the doctor.

This morning I spent at my studies with my tutor, Phaedrus. First I did writing practice on my wax table, some arithmetic and then I had my lesson in public speaking. I did well and Phaedrus didn't beat me. Afterwards, he tried to teach me to play the board game Tabula but it's quite difficult.

I can't wait for my friend Claudius to arrive. We will have a game of knucklebones and play with the dice. Last time he came we played tag and hopscotch and did some wrestling. We made so much noise we disturbed Father. I want Claudius to be allowed to stay for dinner, so this time we will play quiet games.

> Aesculapius, god of medicine, cure Vellibia of her sickness!

> Knuckle bones is a game like our 'jacks'. It was played with the real bones of a sheep.

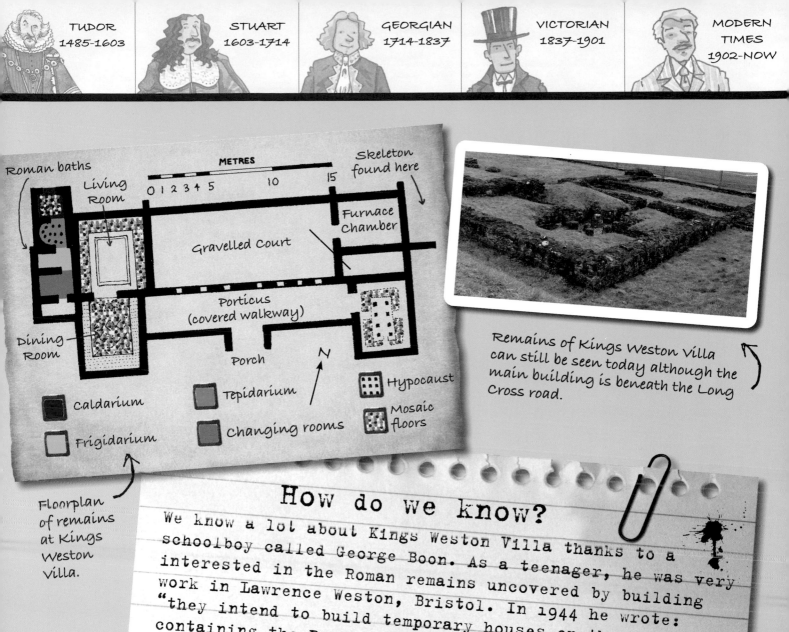

Roman baths

Living Room

METRES
0 1 2 3 4 5   10   15

Skeleton found here

Furnace Chamber

Gravelled Court

Porticus (covered walkway)

Dining Room

Porch

N

caldarium

Frigidarium

Tepidarium

Changing rooms

Hypocaust

Mosaic floors

Floorplan of remains at Kings Weston Villa.

Remains of Kings Weston Villa can still be seen today although the main building is beneath the Long Cross road.

How do we know?

We know a lot about Kings Weston Villa thanks to a schoolboy called George Boon. As a teenager, he was very interested in the Roman remains uncovered by building work in Lawrence Weston, Bristol. In 1944 he wrote: "they intend to build temporary houses on the field containing the Roman remains. Isn't there anything we can do about it? I mean, both the builders, while digging drains and so forth, and the inhabitants of the houses, are absolutely bound to disturb the Roman stuff and certainly find all sorts of things. Once the houses are there, that is the end of our chance to discover anything of value, the layers being disturbed, or even to recover any finds."

In 1948 archaeologists and volunteers, including school pupils, began excavating. They found a main building with lots of rooms. There was a Roman bath-suite, which had been added to as time went on. Mosaic floors stood on stone pillars for hot air to heat the rooms from the hypocaust underneath. They also discovered that the villa had a large living room, a porch and a courtyard - enough space for a big family.

The Market Place

The slave boy stands in the market-place, eyes wide. People come and go, stopping at a stall for an exchange of goods or simply a friendly word. Sometimes a silver penny changes hands. Large wooden carts with leather roofs trundle over the bumps. They are filled with sheep and pigs and grain. Everyone's on the move, except the slaves. They stand in a long row, tied together with rope, waiting for the next stage of their journey.

A Place by a Bridge

Slaves, leather, wool, animal skins, fish, lead, metal and wine were all traded in Saxon times. About 600 years after the Romans left, a Saxon market town grew up between two rivers – the Avon and the Frome – somewhere near today's Castle Park. The Saxons called it 'Brycg stowe' – what we know as Bristol today – which means a place by the bridge.

The two rivers gave the place protection, making a natural moat. The Saxons used the old Roman road between Bath and Sea Mills. Taking goods by river was often easier. Saxon boats travelled along the River Avon to the Bristol Channel and from there to Somerset and Devon.

Slaves

Late Saxon Bristol also traded in slaves. Some slaves were captives taken on raids in Wales, while others were low-born servants of rich Saxon households. Slaves were brought to Bristol from across the River Severn and northern England to be sold at market. They were sent by ship to Ireland and sold to Viking rulers. Many slaves were sold on to Spain and North Africa.

Saxons lived in huts like this one.

...1051 BRYCG STOWE IS MENTIONED IN ANGLO-SAXON CHRONICLE...

'Saturday' is named after a Roman god, Saturn.

The Church

The early Saxons living in Bristol were pagans. They worshipped a different god for every area of life, such as the family, the home, the weather and war. But by the end of the 7th century, England began to turn away from paganism and became Christian, worshipping one God. The Church was very important in the lives of everyday people in Norman times. Fine new churches were built across the town, inside and outside the city walls.

English	Saxon
English	Saxon
Monday	Mona
Tuesday	Tiu
Wednesday	Woden
Thursday	Thor
Friday	Freya
Saturday	Sæternesdæg
Sunday	Sunne

This table shows how the English days of the week are named after Saxon gods.

SPOT THIS!

This was the main Saxon river landing. Can you spot it? Here's a clue: check out Bridge Street near Castle Park.

How do we know?

Monks and scribes kept a written record of England, year by year, called the Anglo-Saxon Chronicle. The Battle of Dyrham between the Britons and the Saxons in AD 577 is recorded in detail and Bristol is listed in 1051. The Anglo-Saxons were warrior-farmers who invaded England from north-west Europe. When the Romans left England to defend their homeland, the Saxons took over the country. According to Saxon law coins could be made only in market towns. Silver coins minted in Bristol are evidence that it was a market town by the 11th century.

Dear God, please can you invent some machine so I don't have to write everything down.

Bristol in Anglo-Saxon times was a river port and the town followed the shape of the River Avon.

9

A King in Chains

All is quiet at Bristol Castle. The day has been busy and the servants are tired. Corbin, the cook's boy, lies on his straw pallet and tries to sleep. But, like everyone else, he is anxious. Even the horses in the stables are nervous. They paw the ground with their hooves. Tonight, the new castle holds a special prisoner – King Stephen. Matilda is fighting him for the crown. Corbin watched the men carry him from his horse, the blood of battle still on his cheeks. And now Stephen lies imprisoned and in chains, somewhere in Bristol Castle, which is one of the strongest castles in the country.

This is what Bristol Castle might have looked like around 1300.

The lucky Bristolians were given the city of Dublin by King Henry II.

In 1141, Stephen was imprisoned in Bristol Castle by his cousin Matilda for nine months!

A Norman Castle

By the time King Stephen was imprisoned in 1141, Bristol Castle was a huge stone fortress. But Bristol's first castle was made of wood. It was built by the Normans to defend their new kingdom. Duke William of Normandy's army had invaded England defeating the Saxon king, Harold, at the Battle of Hastings in 1066. When William became king of England he ordered his knights to build castles as quickly as possible.

The old wooden castle was eventually replaced by a strong stone castle in 1135. By then, Bristol Castle belonged to Robert Earl of Gloucester, a very powerful man. He was helping his half-sister, Matilda, fight her cousin, King Stephen, for the right to rule England. When King Stephen was captured and kept at Bristol Castle there was no hope of escape. However, Robert of Gloucester was himself captured by King Stephen's supporters. The two prisoners were exchanged and King Stephen was eventually restored to the throne. He was the last Norman king of England.

...1135 BRISTOL CASTLE REBUILT...1141 STEPHEN IMPRISONED IN CASTLE...

A Walled City

The magnificent castle meant that Bristol was a well-defended port. By the Middle Ages, Bristol was well-known for its cloth and leather goods, made outside the city walls in Temple and Redcliffe. You can still see part of the city walls in St Nicholas Street and St Stephens Street.

The craftworkers of Bristol formed guilds. Boys could become apprenticed to a guild at twelve years old and learn a trade. They would be taught by their master for 7–10 years. Only guild members could sell their goods in the town. But on market-day, or when the fair came, anyone could trade – and arguments broke out. Every year from 1238 a big fair was held in the churchyard of St James' Priory and spilled into the streets nearby.

A piece of medieval horse poo, now in Bristol Museum, was dug up at Bristol Castle! EUGH!

A New Bridge

As Bristol grew, the old wooden bridge wasn't strong enough to carry the heavy traffic of horses, carts and livestock. In 1247 a new stone bridge was built, joining the Temple and Redcliffe areas to the centre of Bristol. Later in the 1300s the bridge was lined with shops built of timber. At one end stood an arched gateway with the magnificent St Mary Chapel above.

By the late Middle Ages, Bristol Bridge was crowded with shops and houses, some five-storeys high.

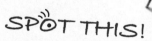

SPOT THIS!

You can explore the ruins of Bristol Castle. Can you spot them? Here's a clue: check out Castle Park near the Galleries shopping centre.

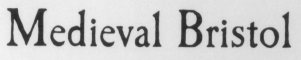
Medieval Bristol

It's noisy down at the harbourside. Everyone's busy. There's hammering and shouting from the men working at ship repairs. Others heave and load great bales of cloth – purple and scarlet and deepest red – onto waiting ships. Barrels of wine tumble off and are lined up at the water's edge. The traveller covers his face at the smell of the cloth fullers, the leather tanners and the soap-workers, and at the dung-heaps along the bank. Time to move on, it stinks!

Hustle and Bustle

By the 14th century Bristol was England's second largest port. Its harbour was bustling, with the smelly leather tanneries and breweries pouring waste into the river. Bristol's streets were dark, dirty alleys. Butchers threw meat remains into the gutters. People emptied their chamber pots into the open channels that ran through the lanes. But Bristol did have clean water that was piped into the town from springs on the higher ground to the north. This meant that Bristolians had fewer stomach upsets than the people of most large towns of the time.

Wormwood, comfrey and vinegar – that should cure you!

Black Death

In 1348 a disease called the Black Death spread to England. Fleas that lived on rats carried the germs on board ships that docked at the harbour. Bristol was one of the first places to suffer. At the time, about 10,000 people lived in the city. One writer of the time, Henry Knighton, tells us: "Almost the whole population of the town perished." People took to their beds, some breaking out in swellings, others sweating, shaking and spitting blood, until they died a few days later. St John's church needed extra land near its churchyard for burying the dead.

...1348 THOUSANDS DIE WHEN PLAGUE COMES TO BRISTOL...

The Merchant Venturers

Bristol recovered quickly from the outbreaks of the plague by attracting people from the surrounding countryside. Merchant 'adventurers' sailed from Bristol's safe harbour to countries such as Ireland, Portugal, France and Spain, trading woollen cloth. They brought back leather, linen, fine wines and dyes. But there were pirates in the Bristol Channel, especially around the island of Flat Holm. The merchants tried to form a guild to protect the city traders from outsiders. In 1552 a Royal Charter allowed them to form the Society of Merchant Venturers. One of the most famous Merchant Venturers was William Canynge who owned a fleet of nine ships and rebuilt the old Saxon church of St Mary Redcliffe. The Merchant Venturers soon controlled the harbour.

Statues of legendary founders of Bristol, brothers Brennus and Belinus, are either side of St John's.

Robert Ricart's map of Bristol in 1479 shows Bristol's four main streets: Broad Street, High Street, Wine Street and Corn Street, with High Cross marking the town centre.

Did you know that St Mary Redcliffe is the tallest building in Bristol?

SPOT THIS!

St John the Baptist's Church is one of four churches which formed part of the walls of the Saxon city. Can you spot it? Here's a clue: check out Tower Lane.

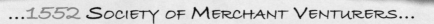

Sea Voyages

The small ship sits bobbing on the water, her rigging jingling in the breeze. Men scramble on board, checking the ropes and pulleys. Crates and packages are stowed away – caskets of salted meat and fish and barrels of foaming ale. There are live chickens squawking and clucking in the hold. The master gives the sails a last-minute check for any rips and tears and the captain unrolls his map. All is ready. The *Matthew* moves off downriver, towed by rowing boats. She will wait in the Bristol Channel until the wind is right for her journey across the open ocean.

> Cabot's £10 reward sounds stingy but it was as much as a labourer's salary for two years!

SPOT THIS!

There is a myth that John Cabot brought back a whale bone from his voyage to give thanks. Can you spot it? Here's a clue: check out St Mary Redcliffe Church.

The Spice Race

In 1497 a wooden sailing ship, called the *Matthew*, set sail with a crew of 18 men. They were seeking a new route to the spice islands of the East Indies. The expedition was led by the Italian explorer called Zuan Cabotto, better known as John Cabot.

Cabot came to Bristol in 1496 where he rented a house in St Nicholas Street. He was backed by Bristol's rich merchants and by King Henry VII, the first Tudor king. At that time, there was a race to find the fastest route to the east by sailing west. Christopher Columbus, backed by the Spanish king, was already ahead.

In May, Cabot set sail in the 23-metre ship, and by 24th June, the *Matthew* landed in Newfoundland, in North America. The land was claimed for England and Cabot was rewarded with £10 and a £20 yearly pension from the king.

...1497 JOHN CABOT DISCOVERS NEWFOUNDLAND...

I hear that Blackbeard lights matches under his hat to make him look fierce!

Rich...

The growing trade with Europe and later with North America made the city's merchants rich. They had beautiful homes out of town, such as Ashton Court which was bought by John Smyth in 1545.

Bristol's strong trading links also attracted pirates. Piracy was illegal but privateering (stealing from other ships with a government pass) was not. Bristol's most famous pirate, Edward Teach, known as Blackbeard, was born near the old harbour. He sailed from Bristol as a privateer to the Caribbean then later became a pirate.

← *Hoefnagel's map of Tudor Bristol.*

...and Poor

But there were poor people in Bristol too. When people couldn't find work in the countryside they moved to Bristol to find paid work. They worked six days a week and earned just enough for shelter, food and clothing. They dressed in rough woollen cloth and lived in crowded, damp houses.

In 1601, Queen Elizabeth made a law to help the poor who were unable to work. It was decided to shelter poor people in 'almshouses' or 'poorhouses' and to train poor children as apprentices. The Merchant Venturers built many almshouses, some of which survive today.

You can still see the Bristol Grammar School at the bottom of Christmas Steps.

New Schools

Red Maids School is the oldest girls' school in England.

In early Tudor times, education was mainly for boys from wealthy families. At the age of 7, boys would go to school to learn subjects like spelling, sentence structure and grammar, and arithmetic. In the reign of Henry VIII, Bristol 'Gramar Scole' was set up by merchants Robert and Nicholas Thorne. It taught Latin, Greek and religion.

Another merchant, John Carr, set up Queen Elizabeth Hospital School, for 'poor children and orphans' in 1590. One of the first schools for girls, Red Maids School, was opened in Bristol in 1634. Daughters of the poor learned to read and sew.

CELT 500 BC	ROMAN AD 43-410	ANGLO-SAXON AD 450-1066	VIKING AD 865-1066	MEDIEVAL TIMES 1066-14

Acton Court, near Bristol, was the home of wealthy landowner and courtier Nicholas Poyntz and his family. King Henry VIII and Anne Boleyn came to stay at Acton Court in the summer of 1535. To prepare for the royal visit, labourers worked for nine months to put a brand new east wing onto the house. Here is an imaginary letter from Thomas, the stable lad, who is 12 years old.

A 'seat' fit for a king: archaeologists have found an extra-large 'garderobe', or toilet, at Acton Court. It was buried in the wall in the king's chambers.

Dear Ma,

There's great excitement in the household these past months. Mr Poyntz heard that the King of England and his Lady Anne will be staying here in the summer. Ever since the news, the place has been in uproar. He's had 350 men or thereabouts working here, felling trees and building. They have torn down the old kitchen block and put up a brand new building where the King and Queen are to stay. There's even a garderobe for the king to do his business!

I do any odd jobs I can, although my proper place is in the stable tending to the horses. I can't wait for the king to arrive. I hope I will get to look after his horses. I don't know if the royal grooms will stay in our servant quarters over the stable block with us. I wonder if I'll be able to understand their London accent?

I hope that you, Pa and the children are well. I am sending with this message the farthing I was given by Mr Poyntz himself.

All my love,

Thomas

I wonder if King Henry will knight Mr Poyntz when he's seen the new privy?

How do we know?

Part of Acton Court still stands today. Scientists can tell how old the buildings are by looking at the tree-rings in the wooden timbers. Tree-ring dating of Acton Court shows that the east wing was brand new in 1535, just in time for the king's visit.

Written records help us, too. We know that Henry VIII visited Acton Court from his own letters and papers. He called it "Mr Poyntz's place". John Leland, writing in about 1540, describes Acton Court, saying it: "standithe about a quarter of a myle from the village and paroche churche in a playne grounde on a redde sandy soyle. Ther is a goodly howse and 2 parks by the howse, one of redd dere, an other of fallow."

Artefacts found at Acton, such as fragile glass goblets from Italy and Spain, are luxury objects – very different from the ones being made in Bristol at the time. They tell us that Nicholas Poyntz was trying to impress and perhaps show that he was a man of the world, like Henry VIII himself.

Henry VIII must have been impressed with Nicholas Poyntz as he made him a knight.

Only the newer east wing of Acton Court is left today.

The Slave Trade

It is a cold January in 1788. The first open meeting of the Bristol Abolitionists has ended, the doors open and people spill out of the old Guild Hall on to Broad Street. Some are tearful, many are angry, others feel ashamed.

"We must make a stand!" urges one lady.

"I will never eat sugar from the West Indies again!" calls another.

Everyone stands around in the cold air, discussing ways in which they can protest. They will sign petitions, collect money, and make badges and banners. The preachers will speak out and the writers will publish. They will print posters and take out advertisements in the newspapers. Everyone – rich or working-class – can play their part. Slavery must be stopped!

The Abolitionists

In the 17th and 18th-centuries, Bristol's port was busier than ever. Ships set off laden with cloth and other goods. They sailed to Africa, where the goods were traded for gold, ivory, spices – and African slaves. Hundreds of slaves were then herded onto the small ships and transported to British-owned lands in the Americas. There they were sold and put to work on huge farms called plantations. The ships returned to Bristol with goods such as sugar, tobacco, coffee and rum, made by slave-labour. Between 1698 and 1807, 2,108 ships left Bristol to trade goods for slaves.

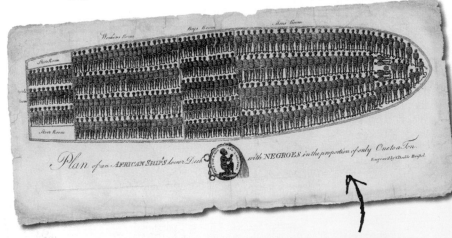

This plan shows how up to 600 slaves were stowed on board a slave ship called The Brookes, in 1788.

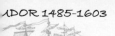 
Bristol's Money

The slave trade made many merchants, like Edward Colston, very wealthy. The merchants and plantation-owners built grand houses, such as those in Queen Square and Clifton. They drank the spa waters at the new Hotwells, and went to balls, the theatre or the races on Durdham Down. Bristol became a fashionable city, second only to London. The enormous amount of money in Bristol caused the first bank, known as Old Bank, to be opened in 1750, one of the first banks outside London. By 1811, there were 13. Today, you can find a plaque of Old Bank on the National Westminster Bank in Corn Street.

> The slave trade was abolished within 20 years of the first protests.

Sugar-loaf City

Trade went on in the coffee houses near Corn Street and in the Exchange, a grand building designed for the merchants. Above the door, statues show European trade with Africa, America and Asia. At that time Bristol's most important industry involved turning the sugar from the West Indies into sugar 'loaves'. Tons of sugar were brought in from the Caribbean. By 1760, Bristol had 20 sugar houses. Other things were made, too: ships, cloth, glass and gunpowder. In 1768, Bristol's old bridge was replaced to take the increasing traffic of coaches and carriages.

SPOT THIS!

This sign records Thomas Clarkson's visit to Bristol. Can you spot it? Here's a clue: look outside the Seven Stars pub in Redcliffe.

Ending the Slave Trade

The Methodist minister John Wesley preached against slavery.

By the middle of the 18th century, many people were starting to think that slavery was wrong. Christian groups, called Methodists and Quakers, wanted slavery stopped. Prominent Quakers like John Harford, a rich banker who built Blaise Castle House, took up the cause. So did a man called Thomas Clarkson. In 1787 he visited the Seven Stars pub in Redcliffe, Bristol, and gathered stories from sailors who worked on slave ships. Clarkson travelled the country showing plans of the overcrowded ships and speaking of the terrible conditions on them. He worked with William Wilberforce in London to make a law against slavery. Ordinary people joined in the protests. There were slave rebellions on the plantations. It took many years but, at last, in 1807 the Abolition of the Slave Trade made trading in slaves against the law.

The New Room in Bristol is the oldest Methodist Chapel in the world, built in 1739 by John Wesley.

John Pinney was a Bristol merchant. He owned sugar plantations on the island of Nevis in the Caribbean. In 1783 he returned to live in Bristol with his wife and family of five children. Pinney had many servants. This is a made-up account by his servant Pero – a real person – who served Mr Pinney for 32 years.

John Pinney's house in Great George Street is now a museum. It is evidence of the great wealth made by Bristol slave-traders.

7 Great George Street, Bristol

I've been serving Mr Pinney now for 19 years. We left Nevis, an island in the Caribbean, a year ago and I am now living with Mr Pinney and his family in Bristol. The sun's always shining in Nevis and sugar canes grow as high as two men! Bristol is very different. It is much colder but I live with the Pinney family and their servants in their grand house. The mistress's maid Fanny Coker is very amusing!

I was sad to leave my sisters Sheeba and Nancy behind in Nevis. But Mr Pinney assures me I will see them again when we next visit Nevis.

Not all slaves are treated well. I have heard about cruel masters who punish their slaves when they don't work hard. Plantation slaves work from sunrise to sunset with only Sundays off and that's if they are lucky. I've heard stories of them running away from their owners.

Mr Pinney is a good master. I have learnt a lot from being his servant. I can shave my master and dress his hair and I can even read – not many slaves can say that!

Pero

Here's your tea, Mr Pinney. Would you like one lump or two?!

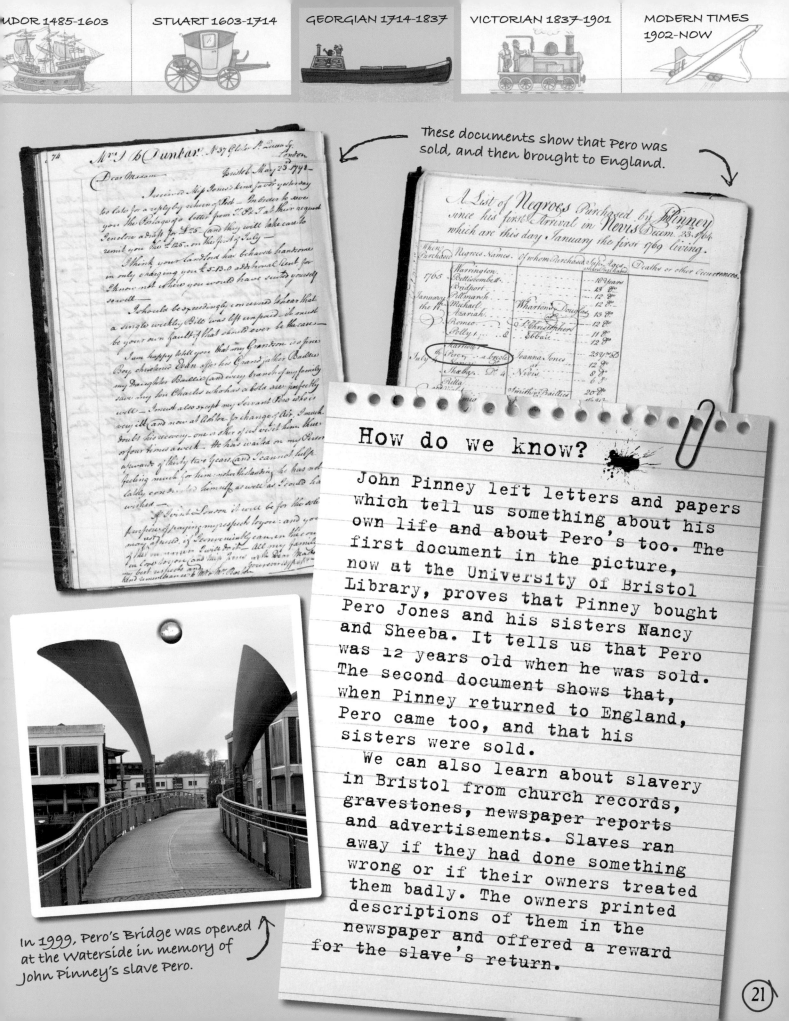

These documents show that Pero was sold, and then brought to England.

A List of Negroes Purchased by Pinney since his first Arrival in Nevis Decem. 23. 1764. which are this day January the first 1769 living.

In 1999, Pero's Bridge was opened at the Waterside in memory of John Pinney's slave Pero.

How do we know?

John Pinney left letters and papers which tell us something about his own life and about Pero's too. The first document in the picture, now at the University of Bristol Library, proves that Pinney bought Pero Jones and his sisters Nancy and Sheeba. It tells us that Pero was 12 years old when he was sold. The second document shows that, when Pinney returned to England, Pero came too, and that his sisters were sold.

We can also learn about slavery in Bristol from church records, gravestones, newspaper reports and advertisements. Slaves ran away if they had done something wrong or if their owners treated them badly. The owners printed descriptions of them in the newspaper and offered a reward for the slave's return.

Further and Faster

It's a bright, cold December day in 1864 for the grand opening of Clifton Suspension Bridge. Bristol is filled with the sound of church bells and guns firing. The crowd standing on Observatory Hill, Clifton, buzzes with excitement. Thousands of people have turned out to watch the procession – it must be a mile long. Flags and banners, ribbons and flowers line the way. Then a great cheer goes up from the crowd. The gates have opened and the first people begin to cross.

Isambard Kingdom Brunel

Bristol's suspension bridge had been a long time in the making. It was designed by a young engineer, Isambard Kingdom Brunel, in 1831, more than 30 years before. The bridge was to stretch high over the muddy banks of the River Avon. At that time it was the longest and highest suspension bridge in the whole world.

In the same year, there were riots in Queen Square. The people of Bristol were worried that the Reform Act, giving more people the vote, would not be passed. Brunel became a special constable during the riots and work on the bridge was halted. Bad weather and lack of money also held up the work on the bridge for many years.

Brunel died five years before the Clifton Suspension Bridge was opened.

Brunel's railway station at Temple Meads connected Bristol to London.

God's Wonderful Railway

Brunel was busy with other projects which would change Bristol and Victorian transportation for ever. At the age of 27, he began work on the Great Western Railway. By 1840 trains ran from Bristol to Bath, and by 1841 they went all the way to London. A grand station called Bristol Temple Meads was built with train sheds, passenger sheds and waiting rooms. We still use this train station today.

...1840 FIRST GWR TRAIN RUNS...1843 SS GREAT BRITAIN LAUNCHED...

SS *Great Britain*

Brunel's dream was to create a fast route from London to New York via Bristol. Brunel designed the steamship SS *Great Britain* to cross the Atlantic Ocean. It was built in Bristol and owned by the Great Western Steamship Company. It was the first 'modern' ship, made of metal, not wood, and driven by a propeller. And it was another record for Brunel: the world's largest ocean-going passenger ship. In fact, when the ship was launched in 1843 it was too big to pass through Bristol's lock system! The ship finally made it out in 1844. In 1845 the SS *Great Britain* crossed the Atlantic in two weeks, carrying 252 travellers.

Whoops, we're stuck! Didn't somebody measure the exit?

Queen Victoria's husband, Prince Albert, arrived in Bristol by train to launch the SS Great Britain.

I won the competition to design Clifton Suspension Bridge. Not bad for a 24 year old!

Bristol Docks

Bristol docks were always busy with ferries and tugs. Large warehouses along the harbour stored goods for trade and manufacture. Soap, tar, anchors, ship's parts – and the first chocolate bars – were all made in Bristol. When Bristol docks became too small for building or handling the largest ships, much of the city's trade was lost to other ports with better deep-water docks, such as Liverpool and Southampton.

SPOT THIS!

This is a statue of Isambard Brunel. Can you spot it? Here's a clue: look around Temple Back East near Temple Meads Station.

Making Connections

Victorian engineering and industry made huge changes to Bristol. The new railways moved people and goods faster than horse-drawn carriages ever could. For the first time, people could escape the crowded city by taking a day trip to the seaside – for the price of a train ticket – to Weston-Super-Mare.

Cholera Epidemic

A feeling of panic has started to spread around our streets. People are saying that the doctors are snatching dead bodies but Pa said it's nonsense talk. One man thinks fireworks will purify the air to make the cholera go away! St Peter's Hospital has had to get more beds for the sick and we are being told to remove all manner of filth from our houses. How can us poor folk do this? At night you can hear people groaning from the pain of the stomach cramps. It's horrible and scary. Cholera has hit Bristol.

Mr Müller educates the orphans so that the boys can become apprentices.

And the girls can become nurses, teachers or go into service.

Bristol's Orphans

Although Bristol was an established city it was still dirty and disease spread quickly. The cholera epidemics left a lot of orphans. German immigrant George Müller came to Bristol in 1832. He was a missionary and wanted to carry out what he believed was God's work. At first, he started an orphanage for girls from his own home at 6 Wilson Street. His plans to care for and educate Bristol's orphans grew and, by 1870, more than 2,000 orphans were living in five of Müller's homes.

This old photo shows crowds gathered at Clifton Zoo for the carnival opening.

INFANT BOYS Nº 1. N.O.H. 16.

This photograph of the Müller orphans was taken in about 1910.

Better Health

Because of the cholera epidemics people began to see the importance of clean water and rubbish collection – and fresh air and exercise. And so Bristol's parks and the Clifton Zoological Gardens were created. The Zoo was a place to meet friends and also see natural history.

Mr Richard Forrest's plan of Clifton Zoo shows walled gardens, lawns and animal enclosures, set around a lake.

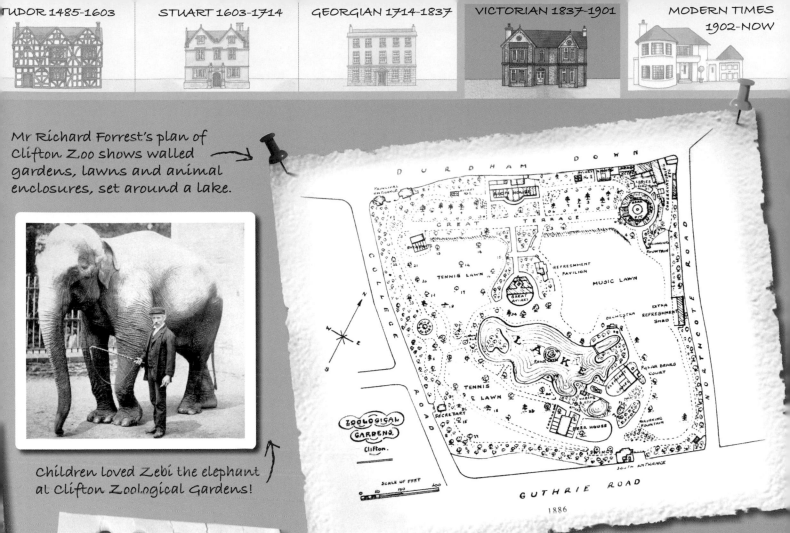

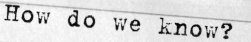

Children loved Zebi the elephant at Clifton Zoological Gardens!

How do we know?

The Bristol Medical Journal is just one source of information on the cholera epidemics in Bristol and tells us how research into cholera progressed and how clean living promoted good health.

One of the most splendid new parks in Bristol was the Zoological Gardens in Clifton, designed by Mr Richard Forrest, a landscape gardener. The Zoo opened to paying visitors in July 1836, just before Queen Victoria came to the throne. As well as beautiful gardens, a day at the Zoo offered animal rides, flower shows, concerts, boat rides, tennis, archery and croquet. An elephant called Zebi arrived in 1868 and was a firm favourite with many children.

The original plans show that the layout of the Victorian gardens was not much different from our modern Bristol Zoo.

Bristol Zoo is the fifth oldest zoo in the world!

25

Bristol at War

Last night the air-raid siren sounded after tea and Mum called us to come quick! We grabbed our gas-masks and ran to the shelter at the bottom of our garden. We could hear the planes flying around and around overhead. Then the bombs came – whoosh, bang! Huge crashes that made the whole ground shake. Mum told us not to be scared but she was shaking too. My brother timed it and the 'All Clear' didn't come 'til gone midnight – six hours we were in that smelly shelter.

In World War Two, Bristol was the fifth most heavily bombed British city.

TAKE COVER

The first air-raid warning sounded over Bristol at 12.15 am on 25th June 1940.

The Bristol Blitz

Blitz, short for 'Blitzkreig', was the German name for the bombing raids on Britain between 1940 and 1941. Bristol was an important target for the Germans. As Bristol was on the west coast, it was ideal for receiving wartime supplies and equipment from America and Canada. War ships were made and repaired in the dry dock in Cumberland Road. Aeroplanes were made in the north of the city, in Filton, Kingswood and Yate.

During the Blitz homes, shops, cinemas, night clubs and businesses were destroyed overnight. Six major air-raids in Bristol killed 1,400 people. When the Blitz began, children from Bristol were evacuated to safer areas. They were sent to the countryside to stay with families and didn't know who they would be staying with.

...1940 FIRST AIR-RAID WARNING SOUNDS OVER BRISTOL...

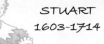

Everyday Life

People had to change the way they lived to survive in wartime Bristol. Everyone carried a gas mask and, when the sirens went, they ran to public shelters or to Anderson shelters in their gardens.

Out in the Atlantic, German U-boats were stopping supplies coming in from abroad. Even food became scarce. People were given ration books to make sure that they had a fair share of the foods that were hard to get hold of, such as meat, eggs and sugar. Parks and gardens were turned into allotments so that people could 'Dig for Victory' and grow their own food. Scrap metal and park railings were collected at 'Metal for Munitions' dumps to turn into guns and ammunition.

SPOT THIS!

This wall was damaged by shrapnel. Can you spot it? Here's a clue: look inside Bristol Museum.

How do we know?

A gas mask from Bristol Museum shows us how people tried to protect their pets from German gas attacks. Its size shows it was made for a cat or a dog. During the war, children and adults were given gas masks and told how to wear them. There were special gas masks for babies, too. But it was a problem for some of the children's pets. Luckily, gas was never used in World War Two.

This photograph of the Museum shows exactly what happened in the air raid of 24th November 1940.

I hope somebody nice picks us.

Gas masks came in only a few sizes, so they would not fit every animal.

This photograph shows the bomb damage at the top of Park Street.

CELT
500 BC

ROMAN
AD 43-410

ANGLO-
SAXON
AD 450-
1066

VIKING
AD 865-
1066

MEDIEV
TIME
1066-1

Bristol Today and Tomorrow...

Today, Bristol is the eighth biggest city in England. We know all about Bristol's past from things people have left behind, such as written accounts, artefacts and buildings. But what about Bristol today? What will we leave for our children and our children's children to discover?

Clifton Suspension Bridge has been closed during the balloon and harbourside festivals since 2003, because it can't cope with the huge volumes of traffic. With roads becoming increasingly busy, will this famous bridge survive into the next century?

In 2008, Bristol became Britain's first 'cycling city' with a 20 km Bath to Bristol cycle route. Will these cycle paths leave clues in our roads and on our pavements for future archaeologists to find?

In 1979, Bristol saw 117 hot air balloons go up, up and away in its first Balloon Fiesta. This festival now takes place every year at Ashton Court and is one of the biggest balloon festivals in Europe. Will balloons still fill the sky over Bristol in years to come?

Every year, in July, hundreds of boats sail into Bristol's harbour, including tall ships, lifeboats and Royal Navy ships. The harbourside fills with musicians, acrobats and other street performers, attracting around 200,000 people. The success of the festival suggests it will continue for a long time yet.

...2009 BANKSY TAKES OVER BRISTOL MUSEUM AND ART GALLERY...

See it. Sense it. Save it

Bristol Zoo isn't just there to show us weird and wonderful animals. It supports research into the protection of wildlife around the world. This work will have a long-lasting effect for future generations.

Bikes, balloons, boats...who needs a car?!

Banksy is a Bristol-born graffiti artist. Some people think his graffiti should be removed but most believe it is street art. Will the outside walls of buildings become the art galleries of the future?

The Cabol Circus shopping centre cost a whopping £500 million to build! It opened in 2008 and has a glass roof the size of one and a half football pitches. Do you think online shopping will eventually replace shopping centres?

The University of Bristol is a leading university in science and research. Will future generations still go to university, as more and more books and other materials go online?

How will they know?

We only have to click onto the Internet to find proof of how we live our lives. We upload pictures, keep blogs and send emails. Will the Internet act as a museum in the future? Should we still keep artefacts for future generations to see and touch? How much of today's Bristol will still exist in 10, 100 or 1,000 years' time?

Glossary

Abolitionist – someone who fought to abolish (stop) slavery.

AD – a short way of writing the Latin words anno Domini, which mean 'in the year of our Lord', i.e. after the birth of Christ.

Air raid – during World War Two enemy planes dropped bombs on Britain. This was called an air raid. To warn people to hide, air-raid sirens wailed out all over the city.

All Clear – when an air raid was over and it was safe again, another siren sounded, called the All Clear.

Almshouse – a place of shelter where poor people could be fed and sometimes trained for work.

Apprentice – at 12, boys could start to learn a trade; while learning, they were called an apprentice.

Aquae Sulis – the Roman name for the city of Bath.

Artefact – another word for an object, often an archaeological one.

Battle of Dyrham – a great battle fought between the Britons and the Saxons in AD 577.

Black Death – another name for the plague.

Cholera – a deadly disease caused by filthy water.

Christian – anyone who believes Christ is the son of God and follows his teachings.

Evacuate – having to leave your home and live somewhere else for safety.

Excavate – to dig into the earth to find things buried there, so we can learn about the past.

Guild – a society of craftworkers and traders.

Harbourside – a place where boats dock to unload their cargo.

Hypocaust – Roman central heating system.

Medieval – another term for the Middle Ages.

Middle Ages – a period of time roughly from AD 1000 to the 15th century.

Pagan – someone who believes in more than one god.

Pallet – a low wooden board used as a bed, often with straw on top of it, for comfort.

Ration book – during World War Two, certain foods were scarce and had to be rationed. Your Ration Book showed how much food you were allowed to buy every week. Once you'd used it up, you couldn't buy any more until the next week.

Royal Charter – written permission from the king or queen to do something.

Scribe – a person who made hand-written copies of books, before printing was invented.

Shrapnel – fragments that break off from bombs or bullets.

Slave – any person who is owned by another. Slaves have no freedom or rights and work for no payment.

Tannery – a building where animal skins were 'tanned', i.e. treated, ready to be turned into goods such as shoes and bags.

Wax tablet – wax, spread on a board, could be written on with a 'stylus' (like a pencil without lead).

Index

Acknowledgements

The author and publishers would like to thank the following people for their generous help:
David Emeney and the Bath Record Office, the George Müller Charitable Trust,
Michael Richardson and the Pinney family, Mike Rowland, and staff at Bristol Zoo.

The publishers would like to thank the following people and organizations
for their permission to reproduce material on the following pages:

Front Cover: The Lordprice Collection; p6: Tracing Tea/shutterstock.com; p8: Diane Earl; p9: Bodleian Library, University of Oxford MS. Laud. Misc. 636, fol. 1r; p10: National Portrait Gallery; p11: Courtesy of the Newfoundland and Labrador Heritage Web Site, Memorial University, St. John's, NL, Canada; p13: Bristol Record Office; p15: Historic Cities Research Project: http://historic-cities.huji.ac.il., The Hebrew University of Jerusalem. Courtesy of Mr.Ozgur Tufekci; p16: Permission of Friends of Acton Court; p17: Permission of Friends of Acton Court; p18: Bristol Record Office; p21: Courtesy of the Pinney Family & University of Bristol Library - Special collections; p22: SSPL via Getty Images; p23: The Lordprice Collection; p24: The George Müller Charitable Trust-Muller House, www.oldukphotos.com; p25: Bristol Zoo Gardens; p26: Bristol Records Office; p28: Amra Pasic/shutterstock.com; p29: Destination Bristol.

All other images copyright of Hometown World

Written by Janine Amos
Educational consultant: Neil Thompson
Local history consultant: Dr Evan Jones
Designed by Stephen Prosser

Illustrated by Kate Davies, Virginia Gray, Peter Kent and John MacGregor
Additional photographs by Alex Long

First published by HOMETOWN WORLD in 2010
Hometown World Ltd
7 Northumberland Buildings
Bath BA1 2JB

www.hometownworld.co.uk

Copyright © Hometown World Ltd 2010

ISBN 978-1-84993-001-7
All rights reserved
Printed in China

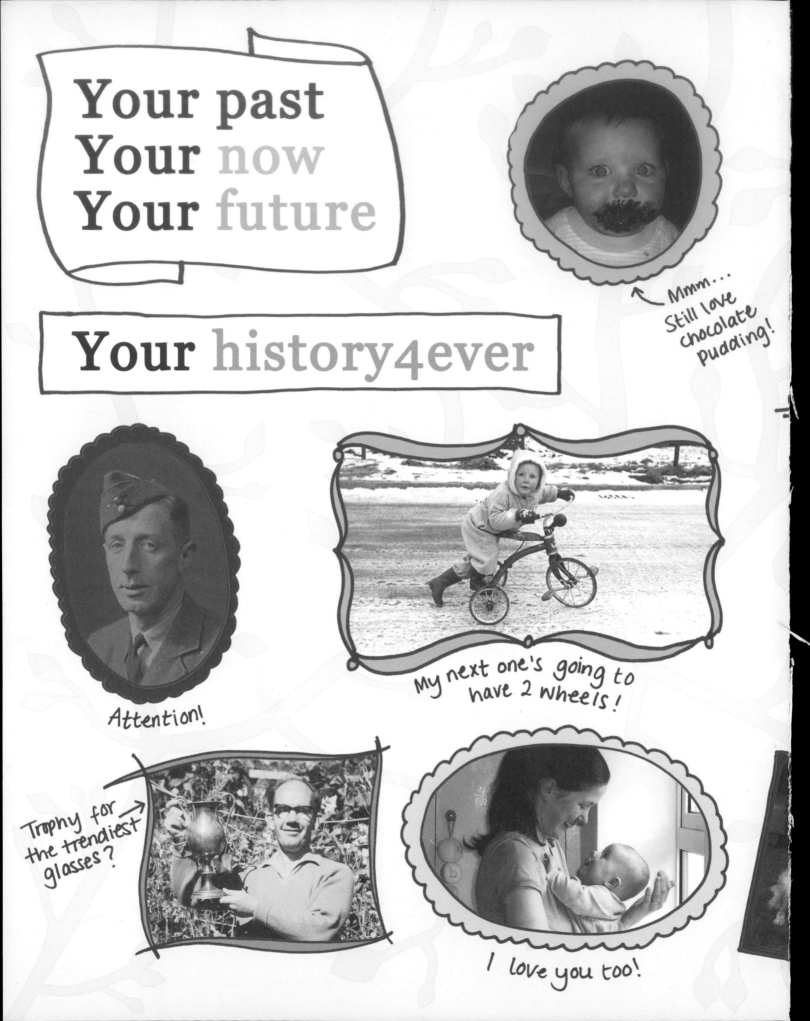